Popular Favorites
BOOK 2

T0081921

Arranged by Fred Kern • Phillip Keveren • Mona Rejino

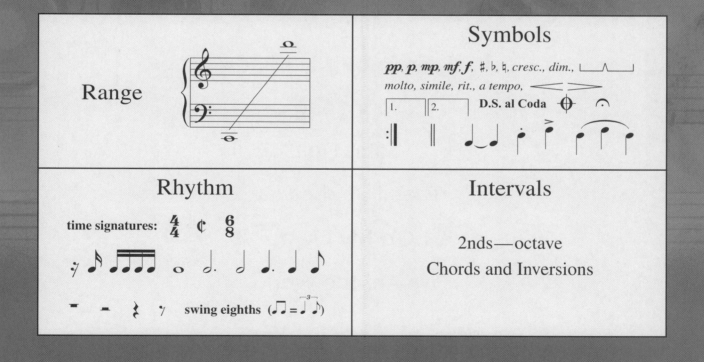

ISBN 978-1-61774-255-2

HAL•LEONARD®
CORPORATION

7777 W. BLUEMOUND RD. P.O. BOX 13819 MILWAUKEE, WI 53213

Visit Hal Leonard Online at
www.halleonard.com

Popular Favorites
BOOK 2

Suggested Order of Study:

The enclosed CD is playable on any CD player.
For Windows® and Mac users, the CD is enhanced so you can access MIDI files for each song.
Simply insert the CD into the disc drive and a window will open automatically
with instructions on how to download the MIDI files.

This product is compatible with Windows 2000 and higher using Internet Explorer, Firefox, and Chrome.
This product is compatible with Mac OS X and Higher using Safari.
(Enhanced features may not be available for Mac OS 9 and earlier.)

For technical support, please email **support@halleonard.com**

Contents

All I Have to Do Is Dream

Words and Music by
Boudleaux Bryant
Arranged by Fred Kern

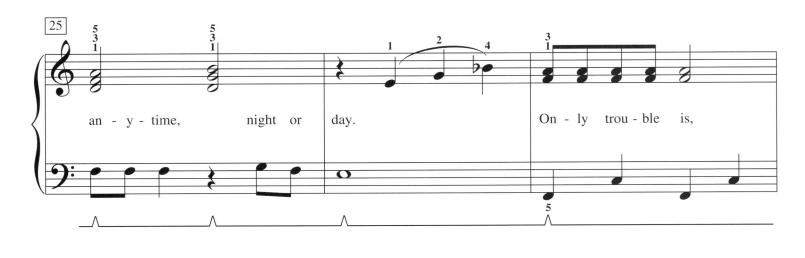

an - y - time,   night or day.   On - ly trou - ble is,

gee whiz, I'm dream - ing my life ____ a - way! _____ I

mf

need you so,   that I could die; I love you so,

and that is why when - ev - er I want you, __ all I have to do is

6

I Just Called to Say I Love You

Words and Music by
Stevie Wonder
Arranged by Phillip Keveren

Moderately (♩ = 120) TRACKS 3/4

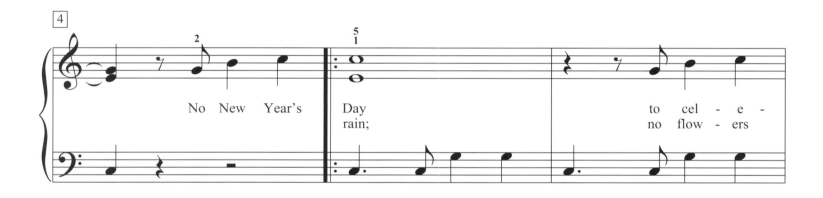

No New Year's Day
rain;
to cel - e -
no flow - ers

brate;
bloom;
no choc - 'late cov - ered can - dy
no wed - ding Sat - ur - day with -

hearts to give a - way.
in the month of June.
No first of spring;
But what it is

no song to sing.
is some-thing true,

In fact, here's just an - oth - er
made up of these three words that

1.
or - din - ar - y day.

No A - pril

2.
I must say to

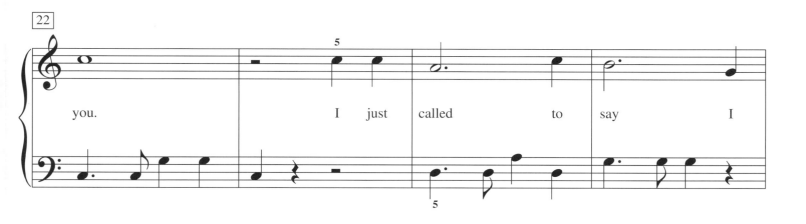

you.

I just called to say I

love you.

I just called to say how much I

care.   I just called   to   say   I

love you.   And I   mean it from the   bot - tom of my

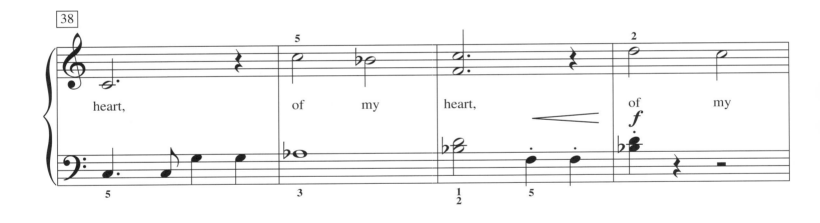

heart,   of my   heart,   of   my

heart. _____

One Fine Day

Words and Music by Gerry Goffin
and Carole King
Arranged by Phillip Keveren

Steady Rock (♩ = 152) TRACKS 5/6

mf

One fine day _____

you'll look at me, _____ and you will know our love was

meant to be. _____ One fine day _____

you're gon - na want me for your girl.

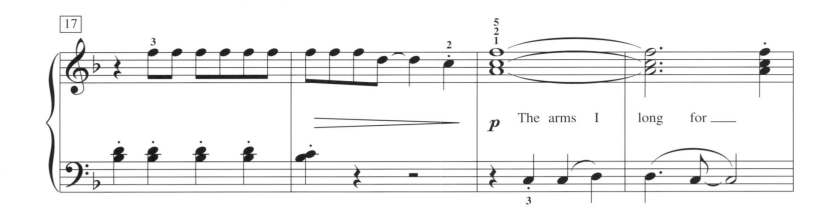

The arms I long for _____

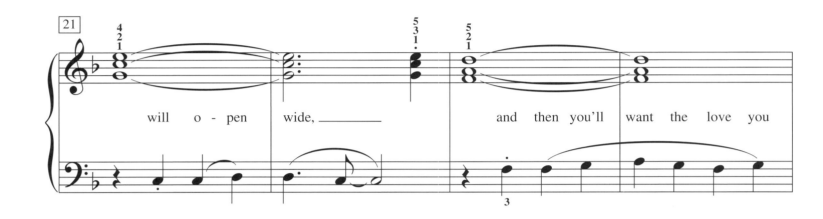

will o - pen wide, _____ and then you'll want the love you

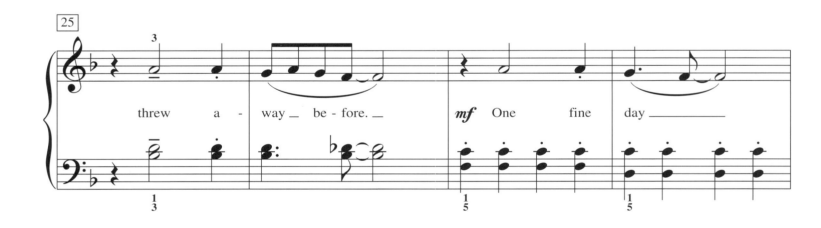

threw a - way _ be - fore. _ *mf* One fine day _____

you're gon - na want me for your girl. _____

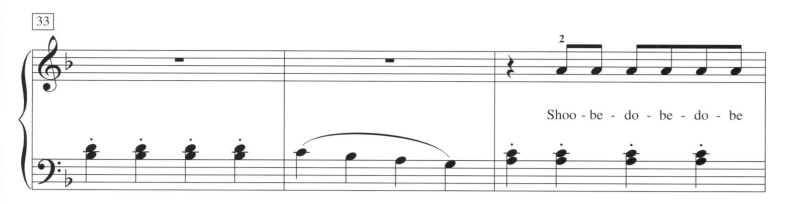

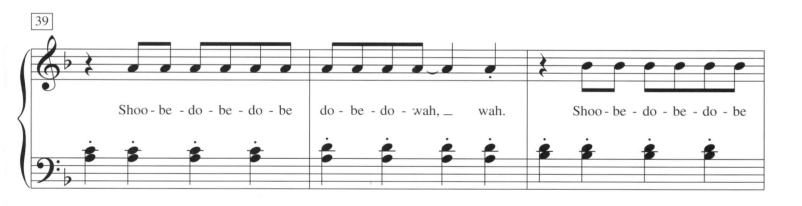

13

I'm a Believer

Words and Music by
Neil Diamond
Arranged by Mona Rejino

Moderately, with a strong beat (♩ = 144)   TRACKS 7/8

mf

I thought love was on - ly true in fair - y tales,
I thought love was more or less a giv - in' thing;

meant for some - one else, but not for me.
seems the more I gave, the less I got.

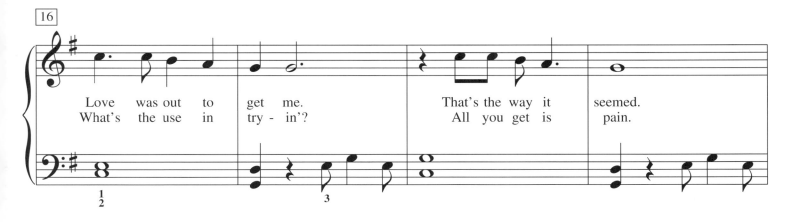

Love was out to get me.
What's the use in try-in'?
That's the way it seemed.
All you get is pain.

Dis-ap-point-ment haunt-ed all my dreams.
When I need-ed sun-shine I got rain.
f Then I saw her

face; now I'm a be - liev - er! Not a

trace of doubt in my mind. I'm in

love.   I'm a be - liev - er. I could-n't leave __

__ her if I tried.

mf

dim. e rit.   mp

Never on Sunday

from Jules Dassin's Motion Picture NEVER ON SUNDAY

Words by Billy Towne
Music by Manos Hadjidakis
Arranged by Mona Rejino

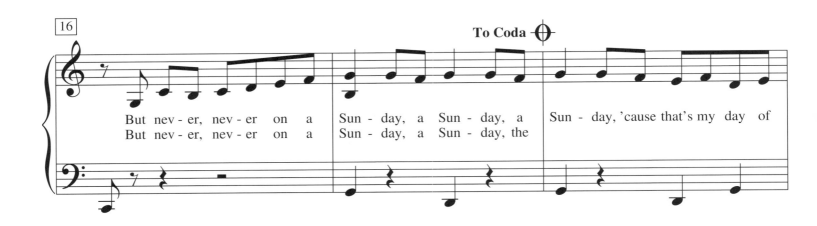

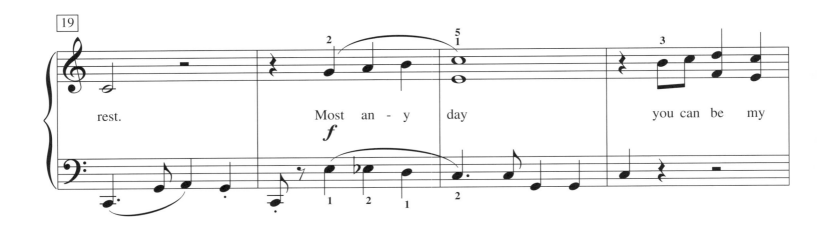

18

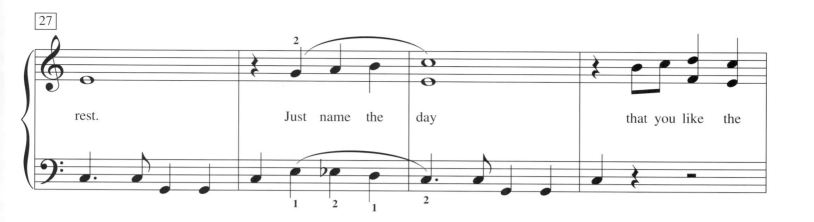

rest.　　　　Just name the day　　　　that you like the

best.　　　　On - ly, stay a - way

D.S. al Coda

on my day of rest.　　　　*mf* Oh, you can kiss me on a

CODA

one day I need a lit - tle rest.

Memory
from CATS

Music by Andrew Lloyd Webber
Text by Trevor Nunn after T.S. Eliot
Arranged by Fred Kern

Freely (♩. = 60) TRACKS 11/12

(Lyrics, measures 5–7)
Mid - night.
Mem - 'ry,
Not a sound from the pave - ment.
all a - lone in the moon - light,

(Lyrics, measures 8–10)
Has the moon lost her mem - 'ry?
I can smile at the old days,
She is smil - ing a -
I was beau - ti - ful

(Lyrics, measures 11–13)
lone. ____
then. ____
In the lamp - light the
I re - mem - ber the
with - ered leaves col - time I knew what

touch me you'll un - der - stand what hap - pi - ness is. _____ Look, a

new day _____ has be - gun. _____ *p*

rit. *pp*

23

Georgia on My Mind

Words by Stuart Gorrell
Music by Hoagy Carmichael
Arranged by Mona Rejino

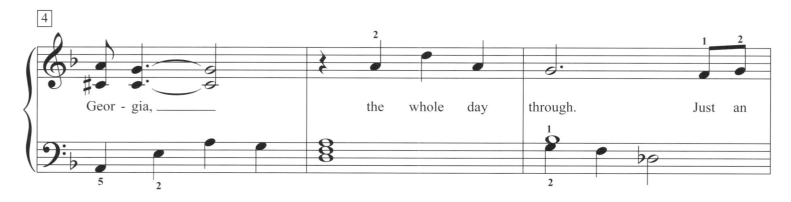

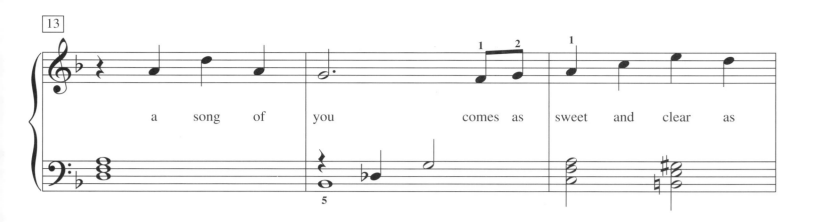

a song of you comes as sweet and clear as

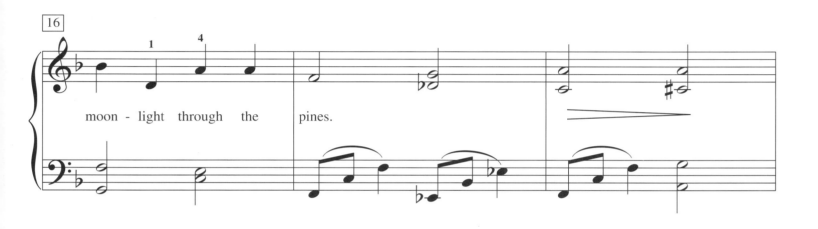

moon - light through the pines.

Oth - er arms _____ reach out to me; _____

mp

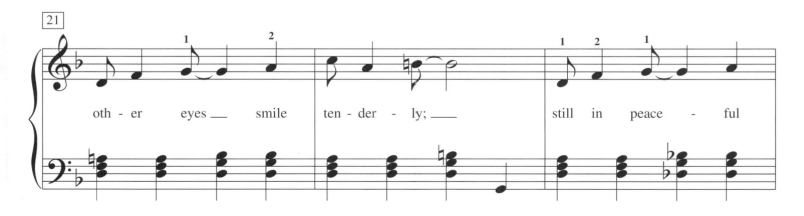

oth - er eyes _____ smile ten - der - ly; _____ still in peace - ful

dreams I see ___ the road leads back to you. ___

Geor - gia, ___ Geor - gia, ___ no peace I

find. Just an old sweet song keeps Geor - gia on my

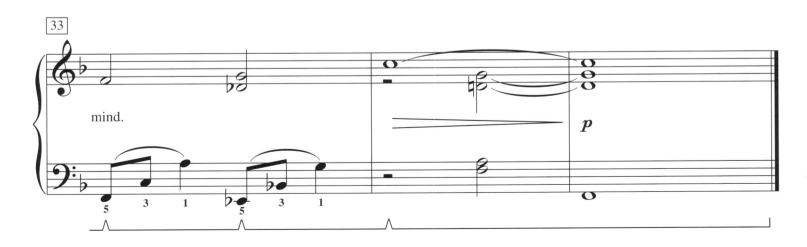

mind.

Satin Doll
from SOPHISTICATED LADIES

Words by Johnny Mercer and Billy Strayhorn
Music by Duke Ellington
Arranged by Mona Rejino

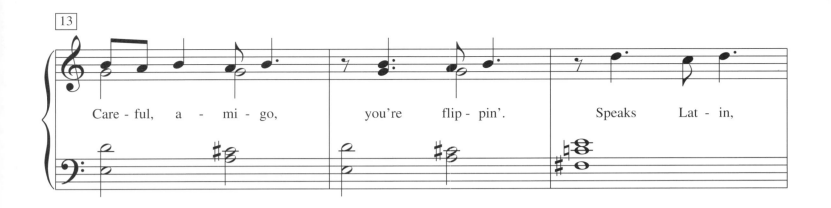

Care - ful, a - mi - go,   you're flip - pin'.   Speaks Lat - in,

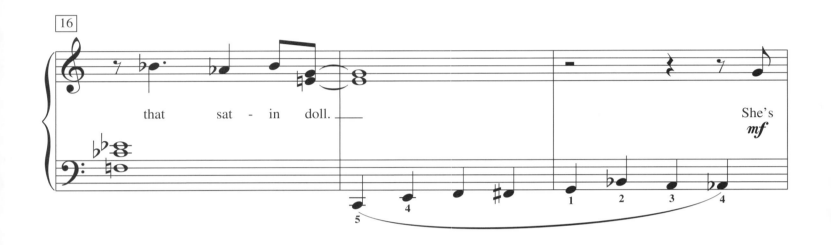

that sat - in doll.   She's

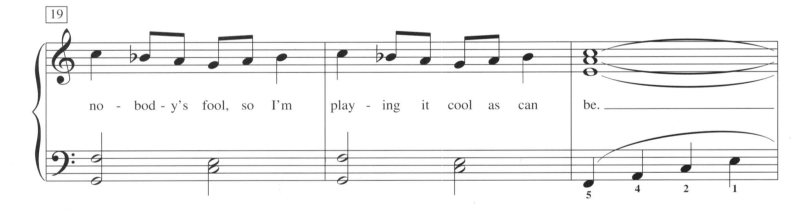

no - bod - y's fool, so I'm play - ing it cool as can be.

I'll give it a whirl, but I ain't for no girl catch - ing

Your Song

Words and Music by Elton John
and Bernie Taupin
Arranged by Phillip Keveren

Pop Ballad (♩ = 60) TRACKS 17/18

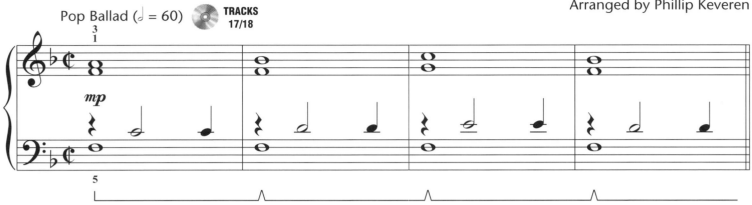

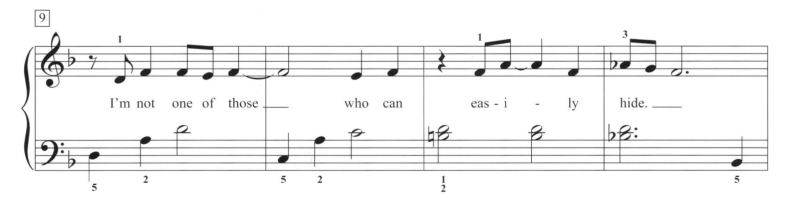

It's a lit-tle bit fun-ny, _____ this feel-ing in - side; _____

I'm not one of those _____ who can eas-i-ly hide. _____

Don't have much mon-ey, _____ but, boy, if I did, _____

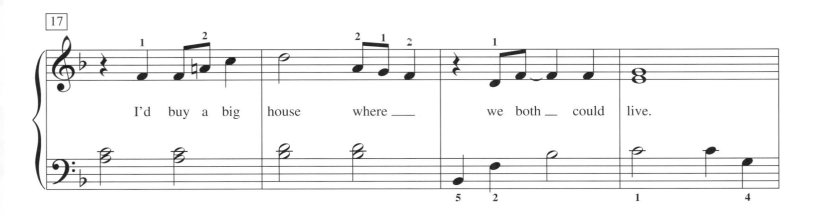

I'd buy a big house where ___ we both ___ could live.

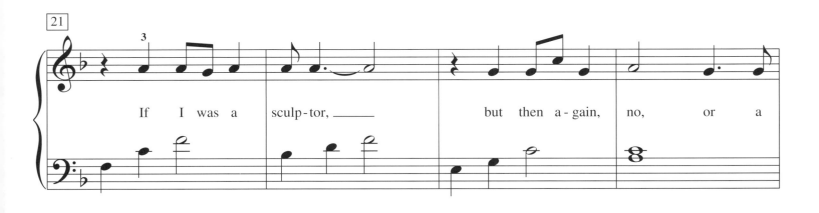

If I was a sculp-tor, _____ but then a-gain, no, or a

man _____ who makes po - tions in a trav-el - in' show, ___

know it's not much, but it's the best I can do, _____

my gift ___ is my   song,   and ___   this one's ___ for   you.

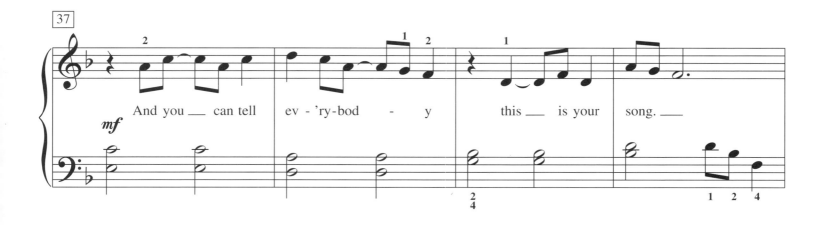

And you ___ can tell   ev - 'ry-bod - y   this ___ is your   song. ___

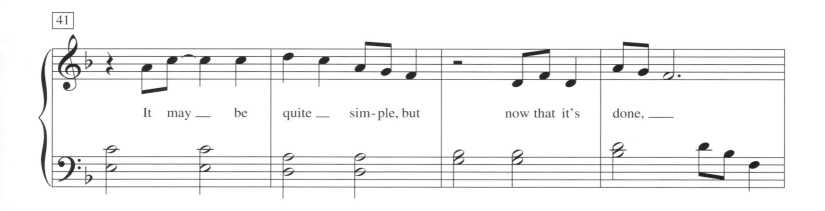

It may ___ be   quite ___ sim-ple, but   now that it's   done, ___

I hope you don't mind,   I hope you don't mind   that I put down in   words   how
rit. e dim.

32

won - der - ful   life   is ____ while   you're _ in   the   world.

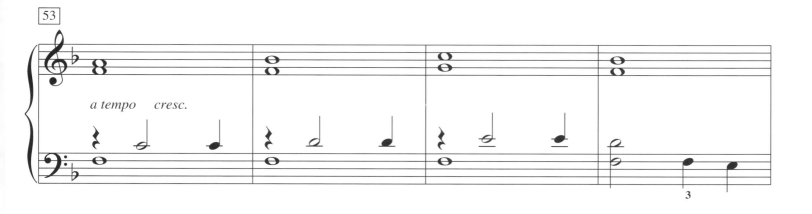

a tempo   *cresc.*

f I hope you don't mind,   I hope you don't mind   that I put down in   words   how

rit. e dim.   *mp*

won - der - ful   life   is ____ while   you're _ in   the   world.

That'll Be the Day

Words and Music by Jerry Allison,
Norman Petty and Buddy Holly
Arranged by Fred Kern

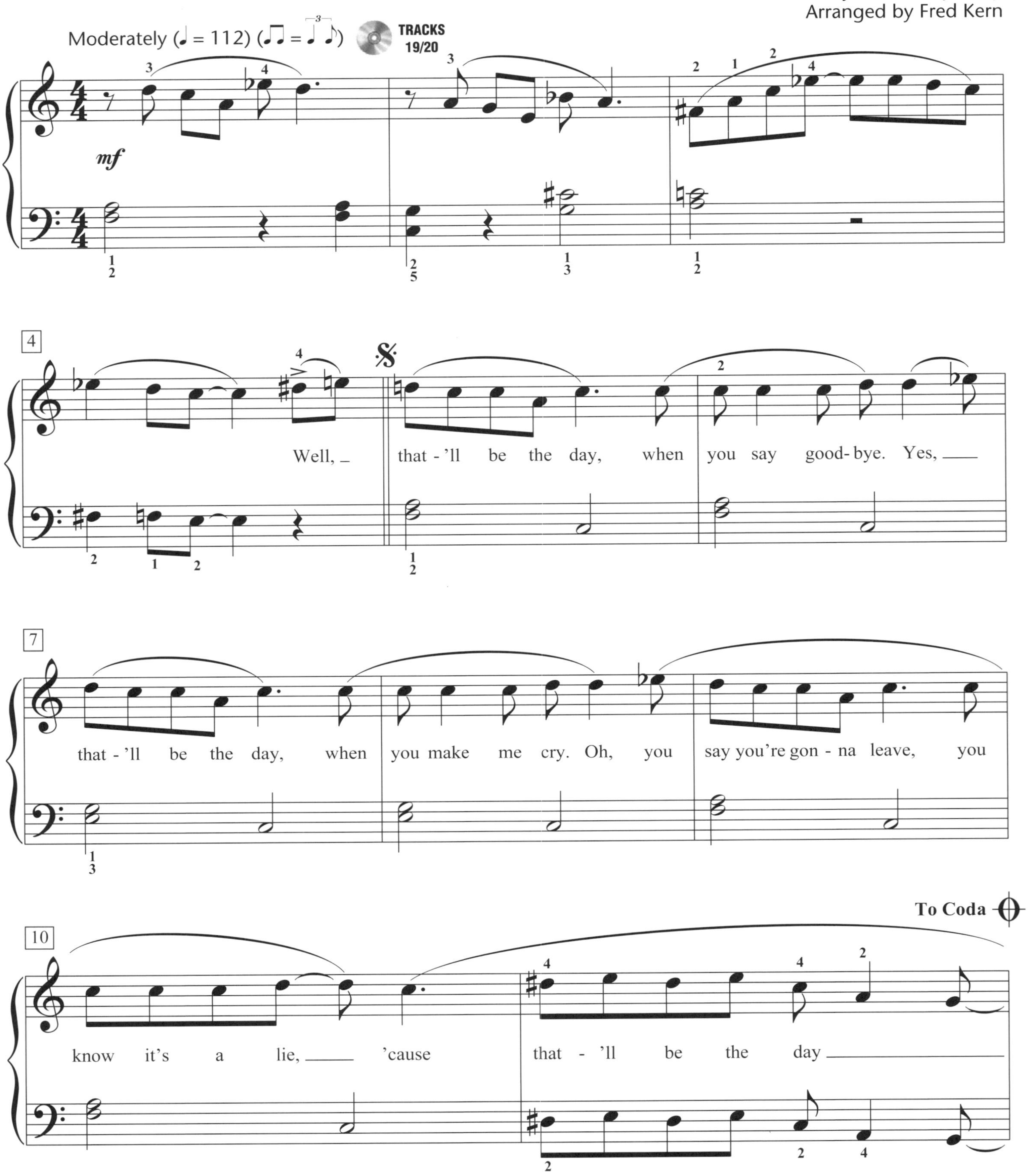
Moderately (♩ = 112)
TRACKS 19/20
mf
Well, _
that - 'll be the day, when you say good- bye. Yes, ___
that - 'll be the day, when you make me cry. Oh, you say you're gon - na leave, you
know it's a lie, ___ 'cause that - 'll be the day ___
To Coda

_____ when I die. _____ Well, you give me all your lov - in' and your

tur - tle dov - in', all your hugs and kiss - es and your mon - ey, too. _____ Well,

you know you love me, ba - by, un - til you tell me, may - be,

that some - day, well, I'll be through! Well, _____ that - 'll be the day, when

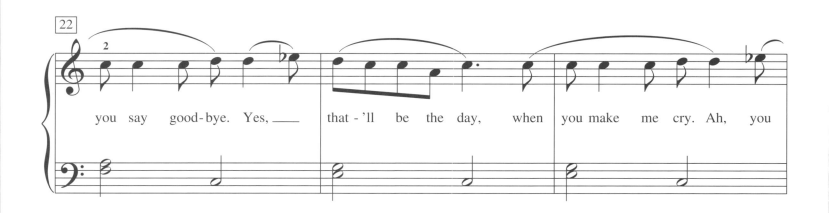

you say good-bye. Yes, ____ that-'ll be the day, when you make me cry. Ah, you

say you're gon - na leave, you know it's a lie, ____ 'cause

that-'ll be the day ____ when I die. __ Well, when Cu - pid shot his dart,

he shot it at my heart. So if we ev - er part and I leave you,

you say you told me and you told me bold - ly, that some - day. well,

D.S. al Coda

I'll be through. Well,

CODA

when I die.

mf

mp

pp

L.H. over $\frac{2}{5}$

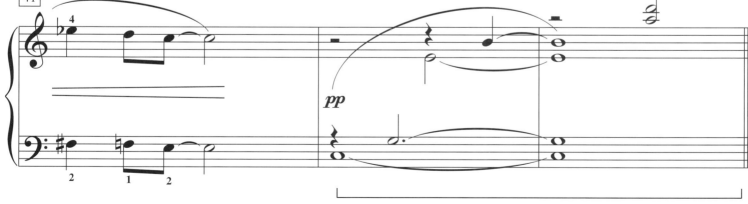

On My Own

from LES MISÉRABLES

Music by Claude-Michel Schönberg
Lyrics by Alain Boublil, Jean-Marc Natel,
Herbert Kretzmer, John Caird and Trevor Nunn
Arranged by Phillip Keveren

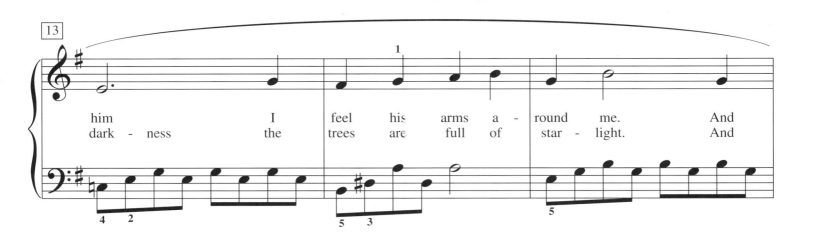

him   I   feel his   arms a - round me.   And
dark - ness   the trees are full of   star - light.   And

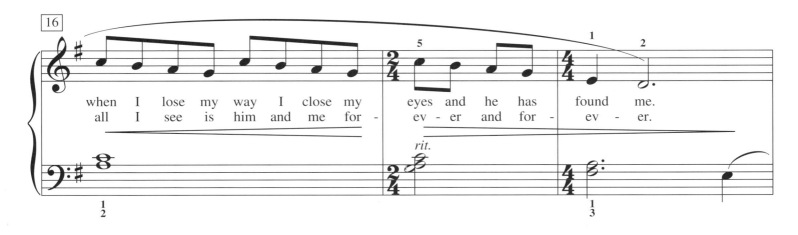

when I lose my way I close my   eyes and he has   found   me.
all   I   see   is him and me for -   ev - er and for -   ev - er.

rit.

1.   2.

In   the   And   I   know   it's

mp a tempo   *mf a tempo*

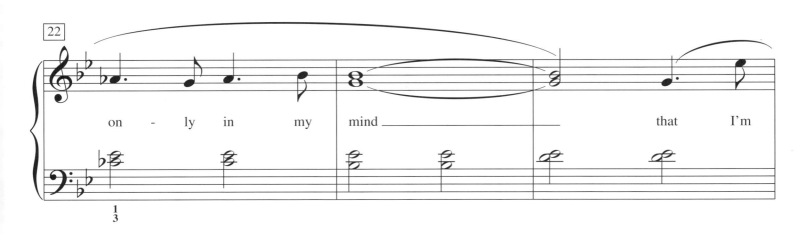

on - ly in my mind _____   that   I'm

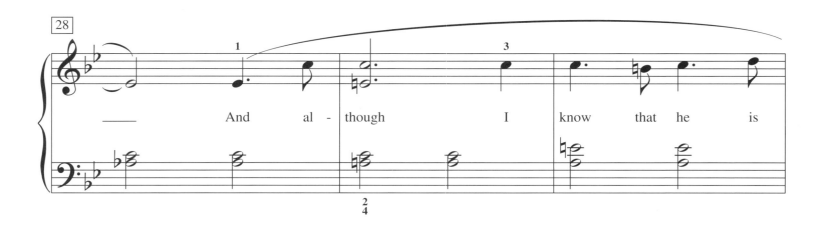

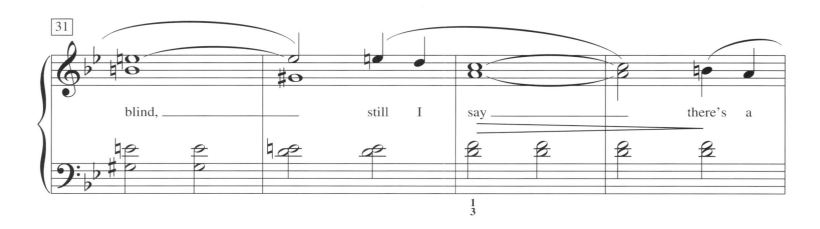

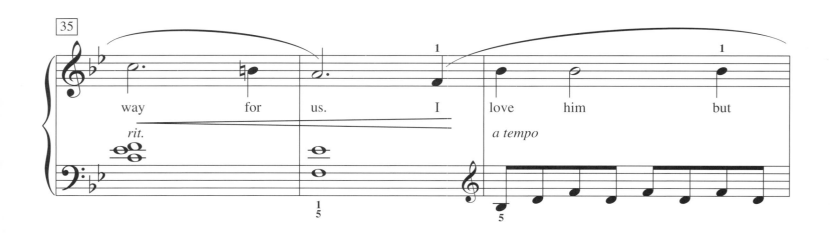

40

when the night is o - ver, _____ he is

gone, the riv - er's just a riv - er. _____

_____ With - out him the world a - round me

chang - es. The trees are bare and ev - 'ry-where the streets are full of

turn - ing. The world is full of hap - pi - ness that I have nev - er

known. I love him,

I love him, I

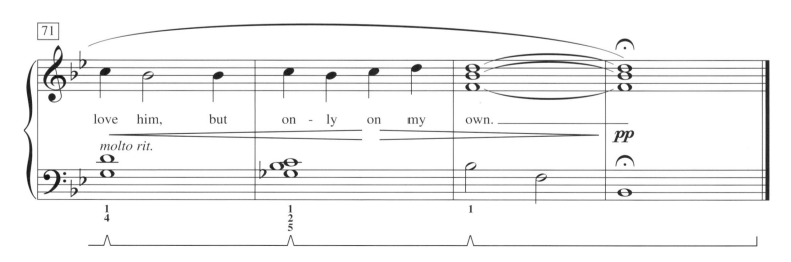

love him, but on - ly on my own.

We Are the World

Words and Music by Lionel Richie
and Michael Jackson
Arranged by Fred Kern

true, we make a bet - ter day, ___ just you and me.

me.

We are the world, we are the chil - dren, we are the ones to make a bright - er day, so let's start

47

giving. There's a choice we're mak - ing, _____ we're sav - ing our own lives. It's time we make _ bet - ter days, just you and me. We are the me. _____